Report

on United Kingdom Implementation
of the Goals agreed
by the World Summit for Children

Presented to Parliament
by the Secretary of State for Foreign and Commonwealth Affairs
by Command of Her Majesty
June 1992

LONDON : HMSO

£5·20 net

Cm 1984

REPORT ON UNITED KINGDOM IMPLEMENTATION OF THE GOALS AGREED BY THE WORLD SUMMIT FOR CHILDREN

Foreword

Children First

Nearly two years ago delegations from 159 states met at the United Nations in New York. Seventy-one heads of state or government took part, making it the largest ever gathering of heads of government. They were brought together by children. Much of the credit for bringing about a meeting on this scale must go to UNICEF.

Meetings themselves do not often achieve much. But they can set work in hand and give that work a push by high-level endorsement. The World Summit for Children did precisely that. The Summit encouraged governments everywhere to take a new look at their measures to help and protect children. All participants undertook the preparation of a plan to implement the goals agreed at the Summit.

Overall, Britain's record is excellent. In education and health, in the plans for a Citizen's Charter, in the reforms we have made in the investigation of child abuse—children's interests shape policy.

The family is the basic unit of our society. Sometimes its stability seems fragile. One parent is often forced to bring up children with no help from the other. We want to change that. We want, for example, to make sure that absconding fathers meet their responsibilities to their children—financial if not emotional. The family must not be taken for granted. It is a guiding tenet of this government's philosophy that policies should, as far as possible, strengthen the family.

Britain's record is, of course, not perfect. But in all areas of apparent weakness—whether levels of still-births or child-care facilities—there is another side to the story. The working group's report brings out this positive side—of work underway, of progress made. But their report will help us target our efforts better in future.

At the international level, which the report also addresses, Britain's growing aid programme, with its poverty focus and emphasis on sustainable social and economic development, helps mothers and children in the Third World, especially in areas such as health care, water supply and sanitation, and education. The Government's commitment to the Summit Declaration and Plan of Action is therefore already borne out by the activities supported through our aid programme. These will continue, as will our strong support for UNICEF as the body most directly concerned with the rights and welfare of children. Together government and non-governmental organisations (NGOs) make a positive contribution to the welfare and development of children.

The report also acknowledges the key role played by NGOs. In partnership with government they carry out many activities for children at home and overseas. Organisations such as the National Children's Bureau, the NSPCC and the Action for Sick Children, alert us to problems, channel voluntary donations and undertake specific projects often on behalf of central and local government. Overseas the ODA funds similar NGO activities through agencies such as Save the Children, Christian Aid, Oxfam and the Catholic Fund for Overseas Development.

We believe that the careful examination recorded in this report shows British policy to be imaginative, sensitive and comprehensive.

REPORT ON UNITED KINGDOM IMPLEMENTATION OF THE GOALS AGREED BY THE WORLD SUMMIT FOR CHILDREN

Introduction

1.   The British Government welcomed the convening of the World Summit for Children in September 1990 and the Declaration and Plan of Action which issued from it. The objective behind the Summit was to give children a better life; there can be few causes worthier than this. That is why the World Summit for Children attracted such extensive and high level support as countries came together to work for this common cause.

2.   Mrs Thatcher, in her address to the World Summit for Children, said that economic progress does not necessarily solve human problems. Her theme was the importance of the family, not only for looking after the material needs of children, but also for giving them " our time, our affection and our wise counsel ". This must be a universal truth, but it is particularly important for the more developed countries not to forget it. The United Kingdom is not burdened in the same way as many countries by the range of problems addressed by the Summit, but nonetheless finds new concerns surfacing which require a different type of approach.

3.   For this, the Government believes that the part played by the State should be complementary to, and supportive of, the role of the family. A stable home environment is the best foundation for the emotional and physical development of children. The Government, for its part, has a responsibility to ensure that the potential of each child is fulfilled by the provision of good education and health services. It also has a special duty to protect children in certain situations, for example where family breakdown occurs or child abuse is suspected.

4.   The United Kingdom's Report adheres in outline to the list of goals set out in the World Summit Declaration and Plan of Action. It also includes under a section entitled " Social Change and Children with Special Needs " some of the challenges to children presented in an industrial society. The second part of the Report examines the United Kingdom's bilateral aid policy in the light of the Summit's goals. It identifies those activities in the United Kingdom's Aid Programme which aim to meet the goals agreed on by the Summit.

PART I: UNITED KINGDOM DOMESTIC ACTION

General

5. As in other developed countries, progress on child and family health in the United Kingdom, when measured by *national* statistics, already equals or surpasses many of the targets set by the World Summit. However, this gives no cause for complacency. The United Kingdom Government is resolved to play a full part in the implementation of the Plan of Action because:

* the setting of goals is seen as a worth-while and productive method of securing public commitment to the promotion of good health and the prevention of disease,

* generally favourable national statistics mask disparities in health status among different groups which the Government is committed to reducing,

* the Government wishes to contribute as effectively as possible to international collaboration on health and social issues including research and development into the prevention and treatment of communicable diseases, the raising of environmental standards and education.

6. The United Kingdom Government attaches particular importance to raising standards of public service by consulting users about their requirements, providing clear information on the services available and encouraging independent evaluation of performance. This has been a constant theme in recent measures taken in the areas of child and family welfare, reinforced by the Government's announcement of a Citizen's Charter.

7. In the development and monitoring of standards of service the Government attaches particular importance to the contribution special interest groups and other voluntary organisations make in representing the views and needs of children and their families. Organisations such as the National Children's Bureau, the National Society for the Prevention of Cruelty to Children and the Action for Sick Children, have long-standing links with Government which have developed into a constructive, mutually beneficial relationship between the State and voluntary sectors.

8. Other relevant Government initiatives have included:

* the Children Act 1989 which provides a comprehensive private and public child care law which recognises that the welfare of the child is paramount while ensuring fairness for parents and emphasising the benefits of family upbringing,

* the support given to preparation of the United Nations Convention on the Rights of the Child. The United Kingdom government signed the United Nations Convention on the Rights of the Child on 19 April 1990 and ratified on 16 December 1991. It welcomes the thrust of the Convention and firmly believes that its widespread international ratification will lead to improvements in the protection of children world wide. The United Kingdom made reservations when ratifying the Convention, the text of which can be found in *Hansard* Vol 201 Column 102 of 17 December 1991. Progress is also being made on ratification of the Convention by the Crown Dependencies and Dependent Territories,

* the reform of the National Health Service which, by introducing a system of contracting for health care, ensured that, for the first time, quality standards for health care are specified in public documents,

* the publication during 1991 of documents on health education and health promotion.

9. The health education and health promotion documents propose a similar approach to that adopted in the Summit's Plan of Action on setting targets for health improvements. The Government will be implementing the health aspects of the Plan alongside its health promotion initiatives. The approach to the specific goals set at the Summit are described in the following paragraphs.

CHAPTER I

Major goals for child survival, development and protection

Child Mortality

10.   Between 1979 and 1989 the infant mortality rate for the United Kingdom was reduced from 15 to 8 per 1,000 live births, and the under-five mortality rate from 16 to 10 per 1,000 live births. These rates are the lowest ever achieved and well below the target levels referred to in the Plan of Action. Nevertheless, infant and child mortality remains a matter of concern to United Kingdom health departments because of the following evidence that further improvement can be attained:

*   mortality rates, while in line with those of European countries at a similar stage of economic development and social composition, remain above those of some Scandanavian countries and Japan,

*   there are variations in mortality rates which show that relatively disadvantaged families, and those from some ethnic minorities, are experiencing higher than average levels of mortality.

11.   The Government has launched a major initiative to reduce the number of stillbirths and infant deaths (deaths within the first year of life), the main features of which are:

*   a system of confidential enquiry into stillbirths and infant deaths is to be established,

*   a major review of the research literature on Sudden Infant Death Syndrome has been commissioned from the Medical Research Council,

*   the National Health Service's capacity to undertake expert post-mortem examinations on stillbirths and infants who die (each region now has at least one paediatric pathologist post) has been increased,

*   regional epidemiological surveys of stillbirths and neo-natal deaths are being established in those regions where they are not currency in operation.

12.   In connection with this initiative, United Kingdom Health Authorities will be looking to improve access to services for certain groups of women and to improve the level of consultant cover on labour wards. They will also be asked to look afresh at initiatives to reduce smoking amongst pregnant women. England and Wales are reviewing maternity and neo-natal services during 1991–92. For 1992–93, Regional Health Authorities have been asked to agree targets to reduce the number of stillbirths and infant deaths and participate in the national confidential enquiry. In Scotland, the Scottish Perinatal Mortality Review Advisory Group was set up in 1982 to develop further the work of the Scottish Perinatal Mortality Survey which had been carried out on a research basis since 1977. Since 1982, a report on Scottish Stillbirth and Neo-natal Deaths has been published as an epidemiological survey. The Advisory Group is currently undertaking a 2-year inquiry into the intrapartum and neo-natal deaths of normally formed babies weighing 2,500g and over in order to identify deficiencies in clinical care, including equipment, staffing and record-keeping. The United Kingdom Government will be looking to these measures to secure a reduction in infant mortality in line with the guidelines agreed at the World Summit for Children.

13.   The mortality rate for children aged one to five in the United Kingdom is much lower than that for infants, but the Government is committed to action to reduce both mortality and morbidity in this age group. The main causes of illness and death are accidents, cancer and respiratory infections, with a reported increase in the incidence of asthma giving particular cause for concern. The health education and health promotion documents mentioned earlier variously include references to accidents, cancer and asthma and any targets identified for health improvements in these areas would be relevant to reducing mortality in childhood.

218490   C*

Maternal Mortality

14. In the United Kingdom maternal deaths are defined to include:

* " direct " deaths resulting from obstetric complications of pregnancy, labour and the puerperium,

* " indirect " deaths resulting from a previous disease, or a disease which developed during pregnancy and was aggravated by pregnancy,

* " fortuitous " deaths resulting from causes not related to, or influenced by, pregnancy.

15. In the three years 1985 to 1987 a total of 174 maternal deaths were recorded. This represented a reduction in the maternal mortality rate over the previous triennial period (1982 to 1984) from 9·3 deaths to 7·6 deaths per 1,000,000 births. This figure compares favourably with the rates achieved elsewhere in Northern Europe and a further reduction in the order envisaged in the Plan of Action is not practicable. However, there remains particular concern about the two most frequent causes of maternal death—high blood pressure in pregnancy and pulmonary embolism—and emphasis is being placed on the need to have expert teams available to treat hypertensive disorders.

16. An important contribution to the low level of mortality now experienced in the United Kingdom has been made by the Government's policy for improving maternity services, including the confidential enquiry into maternal deaths which has been in operation in England and Wales since 1952, in Northern Ireland from 1956 and in Scotland from 1965. The continuation of this enquiry and the incorporation of the results into training and good practice, as well as the other measures referred to for the improvement of maternity services, will ensure that maternal health remains central to the Government's health strategy.

CHAPTER II

Women's Health and Education

17. The United Kingdom Government attaches high priority to promoting women's health and ensuring they have equal opportunities in education and employment. Relevant policies are taken forward in consultation with the Women's National Commission, an advisory committee set up in 1969 with 50 women members drawn from national organisations with large and active memberships of women.

18. The Department of Health has published a women's health booklet: " Your Health— A Guide to Services for Women ". It draws together in a single publication brief details of the main health services which are available to women and encourages them to make full use of them, especially the many preventative services such as breast and cervical cancer screening. It also shows where more information can be obtained on a range of issues in the form of leaflets, telephone advice lines or organisations to contact. Similar booklets are to be issued in Wales, Scotland and Northern Ireland.

19. A book of advice to families on health and welfare in pregnancy is given free of charge to all newly-diagnosed pregnant mothers in the United Kingdom. It contains guidance on healthy eating, food handling and preparation.

20. It is the United Kingdom Government's policy to support and promote breastfeeding as the best means of nurturing infants of both sexes. Measures to implement this policy are underpinned by the steps the United Kingdom has taken to achieve the aims and principles of the WHO International Code on the Marketing of Breast-Milk Substitutes and the WHO Resolution seeking to ban the provision of free and low-priced supplies of infant formulae to hospitals and clinics.

21. Since 1975 there have been quinquennial surveys of infant feeding practice covering the first nine months of life. The early surveys showed an increase in the prevalence and duration of breastfeeding. The 1985 Survey indicated that this trend had ceased. As a result, the Government initiated discussions that led to the formation of the Joint Breastfeeding Initiative (JBI). The JBI brings together representatives of the voluntary organisations that support breastfeeding and the relevant health care professions. The JBI aims to increase breastfeeding rates through professional and public education and

increasing its social acceptability. The results of infant feeding surveys that began in August 1990 will help assess progress made. Although the United Kingdom Government's policy is to support and promote breastfeeding, support is also given to mothers who choose not to breastfeed.

Family Planning

22. In the United Kingdom health education includes sex education and advice about health risks in the pre-conception period. There is also a wide range of family planning services.

23. The National Curriculum Council (NCC) has identified health education (including sex education) as a major cross-curricular theme contributing to pupils' personal and social development. The NCC's document "Curriculum Guidance 5: Health Education" issued to all primary and secondary schools in September 1990 identifies education for family life and sex education as two key areas which pupils should study at all stages of their school careers. It also suggests the types of issue to be covered at each stage and how these might be integrated into the wider curriculum. In Scotland during 1990 the publications "Promoting Good Health—Proposals for Action in Schools" and "Health Education in Scottish Schools—an Introduction for Parents" were launched. The first of these was aimed at enabling schools to consider the promotion of health in the total life of the school, and the parents' booklet aimed at encouraging the partnership between parents and schools. Health education is also a cross-curricular theme, and a statutory part, of the Northern Ireland Curriculum.

24. Information collected centrally indicates that in the United Kingdom some 4·5 million people make use of National Health Service family planning services. The service is available free of charge from general practitioners (over 90 per cent of GPs now provide contraceptive services) and clinics run by health authorities and voluntary organisations. People are free to choose their source of advice. The Government is now spending over £100 million per year on family planning services. In addition, about £1 million in central funding is being provided to voluntary organisations for work in the family planning field, eg to improve information about family planning and sexual health.

Maternal Care

25. The British Government recognises that to have the best chance of a healthy and successful pregnancy, women should be encouraged to make early and regular use of ante-natal care services. Most women visit their general practitioner for confirmation of pregnancy and to make arrangements for subsequent ante-natal care. Ante-natal care is provided by hospital obstetricians, general practitioners, and community and hospital midwives.

26. The Government believes that women should be encouraged to have babies in a maternity unit which can offer a range of obstetric, paediatric and supporting services necessary to cope with an emergency. These facilities can be provided in a consultant unit under the care of a consultant or in a general practitioner unit adjacent to a consultant unit. During pregnancy the responsibilities of the midwife and doctor are inter-related and complementary. Normally the midwife will be the key person supporting the woman with medical care available if needed. In every consultant unit there should be a doctor immediately available to the delivery suite, and a consultant obstetrician or his deputy should be available to take over from junior medical staff when necessary.

CHAPTER III

Nutrition

27. In the United Kingdom the mother of each newborn child receives, free of charge, a copy of the Health Education Authority publication "Birth to Five"—a guide to the first five years of being a parent. The section on feeding the family advises on how to provide children with a varied diet which should contain all the nutrients they require whilst warning of the danger of an excessive intake of sugar or fats. The introduction of healthy eating in childhood is recognised as an important determinant of adult life-style and health. To increase knowledge and information in this area the Chief Medical Officer's

218490   C*2

Independent Committee on the Medical Aspects of Food Policy has, for the first time, set up a group to look at malnutrition of young children during the weaning period. In addition, and as part of a programme of nutritional surveys that will eventually cover all population groups, a major dietary and nutritional survey of children between the ages of one-and-a-half and four-and-a-half will begin shortly. The Welfare Food Scheme helps families in receipt of Income Support by the provision of milk and vitamins free of charge.

Low Birthweight

28.   Over the period 1984 to 1988 in the United Kingdom, it is estimated that 39,500 babies were born at a weight below *1·5* kg out of total births of 3,808,500—a proportion of 1 per cent. This reflects the high standards of maternity care now being achieved in the United Kingdom, but the Government recognises how critical birthweight is to the survival and future health of the child and one of the objectives of its initiative to improve the quality of maternity care (see paragraphs 13–15 and 24–25)—including standards of pre-conceptual and ante-natal care—is to reduce the number of low birthweight babies.

Nutritional Deficiencies

29.   The Dietary and Nutritional Survey of British Adults published in 1990 showed that average intakes of iron from food sources in women—particularly young women—were below recommended levels. Health education advice issued to schools stresses the need for a balanced diet. It is also a standard procedure to test pregnant women for anaemia and, where it is diagnosed, appropriate treatment is prescribed. On the other hand, iodine deficiency disorders due to malnutrition are very rare in the United Kingdom. Vitamin A deficiency is not a problem in the United Kingdom, but there is concern about the suggestion that *excessive* consumption of vitamin A is a possible cause of birth defects. The Chief Medical Officers in the United Kingdom issued advice in October 1990 cautioning women who are, or may become, pregnant to avoid any dietary supplements including tablets and fish liver oil drops containing vitamin A except on medical advice. Such women were also advised, as a matter of prudence, not to eat liver. The cause of high levels of vitamin A in animal liver is being investigated to see whether changes in animal feeding practices could reduce these levels.

Growth Promotion

30.   A comprehensive child health surveillance programme is provided in the United Kingdom. It starts with an examination by a paediatrician close to birth and continues with a series of screening tests and developmental checks at around six weeks, eight months, 21 months, 39 months and five years. Rate of growth plays an important part in this programme and is estimated by calculating the increase in height over a specific time interval. The calculated figures are plotted on a chart showing the percentiles for average rates of growth and, sometimes, the range in which referrals should be considered. A Report " The Diets of British Schoolchildren ", published in 1989, showed that intakes of nutrients for nearly all children across all social classes were adequate and their rate of growth appropriate to their age. These findings are confirmed and supported by information obtained in the government-sponsored " National Study of Health and Growth ".

CHAPTER IV

Child Health

Serious Illness and Immunization

31.   The United Kingdom Government is committed to securing the eradication of poliomyelitis through international co-operation, not only among statutory agencies, but through Rotary International, with the support of voluntary organisations concerned with family and child welfare. Here promising progress has already been made in that there have been no reports of wild virus polio cases for four years and work is in hand to produce the evidence which will lead to a WHO certificate of elimination in the United Kingdom. Elimination of neo-natal tetanus has already been effectively achieved. In 1990, for the first time since records began in 1940, not one death from acute measles was reported in the United Kingdom. The Government hopes to maintain this record and has set a target reduction in the incidence of measles of 90 per cent by 1995 in the 26,000 cases reported in 1989.

32.   Diarrhoea is not a significant cause of death or serious illness among children in the United Kingdom. The Health Education Authority " Birth to Five " booklet advises of the danger of dehydration from diarrhoea in young babies and the need to seek medical advice.

33.   Uptake of immunisation in the United Kingdom has now exceeded 90 per cent for diptheria, tetanus and polio by 18 months of age, 85 per cent for pertussis (whooping cough) by the same age, and 90 per cent for measles, mumps and rubella combined vaccine by 24 months. The targets for these diseases set in the Declaration and Plan of Action should, therefore, be achievable but the Government remains concerned about disparities in take-up between localities. It is targeting promotion of immunisation at population groups with low take-up rates. Tuberculosis (BCG) immunisation policy in the United Kingdom targets not only high risk infants, but all school children at ages 10 to 13. Reinforcing doses of tentanus vaccine are recommended for adults.

Respiratory Infections

34.   Deaths from diseases of the respiratory system among children below five years in 1988 in the United Kingdom totalled 472, of which 389 occurred in infants under one year. The United Kingdom Government is concerned to see this relatively low level of mortality reduced and for England and Wales has identified asthma as an area in which targets might be set for health improvements as part of its health strategy. A close interest is being taken in research into the effect environmental conditions have on respiratory disease in children. Starting from such a low baseline a reduction of the order of one third in present rates of mortality may not be practicable, but the Government will continue efforts to reduce the burden of respiratory disease particularly among infants.

CHAPTER V

Water and Sanitation

Safe Drinking Water

35.   Adequate supplies of high quality drinking water have long been generally available in the United Kingdom. About 99·3 per cent of the residential population receives mains public water supplies. Steps are being taken to ensure that the quality of water from non-mains sources is satisfactory. Grants are available towards the cost of connecting the small proportion of the rural population still without a mains supply, where this is a feasible option.

Excreta Disposal

36.   Over 95 per cent of the residential population of the United Kingdom is connected to a public sewer. Grants are available in England and Wales to assist with the cost of connection in rural areas. In 1990–91 grants totalling £5·9 million were paid for connecting rural properties in England to mains water and sewerage. In Scotland a new £130 million Sewerage Improvement Grant was introduced in 1991 for works on sewerage, sewage treatment and disposal to reduce pollution or otherwise benefit the environment. Mains connection has the advantage over other methods of disposal in ensuring that the final disposal of waste takes place in an environmentally acceptable manner. The problem of water pollution resulting from discharges from septic tanks was highlighted in a report, published by the National Rivers Authority (NRA) in July 1990, which suggested that in sensitive receiving areas no such discharges to the soil should be permitted except with the specific consent of NRA.

CHAPTER VI

Basic Education

Parent's Charter

37.   The Government has published separate Charters for parents in England, Wales and Scotland as part of its drive to improve general standards of education in schools and colleges. A separate Charter is in preparation for Northern Ireland. The Charters aim to

increase parents' involvement in their children's education by improving the information available to them and setting out clearly their rights and responsibilities as parents. The aim is that all parents of school age children should receive a copy of the appropriate Charter.

38.   The Charters set out parents' existing rights and explain the Government's plans to give them new rights to information. These are an annual report on their child's progress at school and, for England and Wales, regular reports by independent inspectors on the strengths and weaknesses of schools, together with published tables comparing the performance of local schools and colleges in terms of public examination and national test results, truancy rates and the destinations of school leavers.

Pre-School Care

39.   There is a wide range of services for children under five, particularly those who are approaching the years of compulsory schooling. These include nursery classes, admission when children are four to primary classes, and day care in playgroups, in day nurseries or with childminders. Playgroups, which are usually part-time, are commonly run by voluntary bodies. Day nurseries may be run by voluntary organisations or private businesses. Childminders are normally self-employed. Otherwise day care facilities are mostly private. The numbers of under fives (chiefly three and four year olds) attending school, full-time or part-time, in the United Kingdom have been increasing steadily (from 44 per cent in 1981 to 49 per cent in 1989). Overall, over 90 per cent of three and four year olds now take part in some form of group activity with their peers—part-time or full-time.

40.   However, choice between alternative forms of provision is limited in some areas. The Government is encouraging growth through the annual grant settlements to local authorities. New legislation (the Children Act 1989) also gives social services and education departments in England, Wales and Scotland a duty to review the pattern, level and future provision of day-care services in their area and publish a report. The Government is promoting the educational content of day care facilities. Measures include grants to expand the staff training programmes of the Pre-school Playgroups Association (and the corresponding Scottish Association), to which the majority of playgroups are affiliated. Recent legislation enables social service departments to seek help from local education authorities in the exercise of their duty in regulating private and voluntary day care services and childminding. In Northern Ireland, the Government gives grants to the Northern Ireland Pre-School Playgroups Association. The forthcoming Children (NI) Order will bring Northern Ireland child care law broadly into line with the Children Act and will include a duty to review day care services.

Compulsory Education

41.   Free, compulsory, universal education begins in the United Kingdom at the age of five; in Northern Ireland, children of four years and two months and over are required to begin formal schooling in the following September. In Wales, primary (and secondary) state education is also available through the medium of Welsh. Additionally, it is a statutory requirement that Welsh be taught as a subject in state schools.

42.   Grants payable under Section 11 of the Local Government Act 1966 are being used to remove barriers to true equality of educational opportunity for ethnic minority groups, where mainstream programmes alone are insufficient to remove those barriers. The majority of funding provides support for teaching English as a Second Language, whilst provision is also made for projects designed to raise achievement, strengthen ties between schools and parents, and provide other special support to ethnic minority children. Such grants enable, for example, specialist teachers to be employed in schools to help children whose mother tongue is not English to gain access to the curriculum and to benefit equally from educational opportunities. In the 1990–91 financial year some £108 million was paid through Section 11 grants in support of expenditure across all phases of education.

Adult Illiteracy

43.   There are very few adults in Britain who cannot read or write at all, but there are substantial numbers (estimated at around 5·5 million) who cannot cope with the demands of everyday life. They cannot, for example, fill in forms, check pay-slips or give the correct

change. The illiteracy rate is higher in men than in women and there is therefore not a need for a special focus on women. To help prepare young people for adult life the Government is taking strong action to raise standards of literacy in schools through the introduction of the National Curriculum, in which English is a core subject. Statutory attainment targets and programmes of study in English are being introduced progressively. These measures mean that pupils and teachers have clear objectives from the outset in the basic skills of reading, writing, speaking and listening, with a structured approach to the teaching of punctuation, spelling and grammar. The introduction of assessment at regular intervals means that children having problems will be identified at an early stage and appropriate help can be given.

44.   The Adult Literacy and Basic Skills Unit (ALBSU), which advises the Government, acts as the central focus for adult literacy and related basic skills in England and Wales. The equivalent body for Scotland is the Community Education Service. Grants to ALBSU have increased more than six-fold over the past decade to over £3 million in 1991–92. Local Education Authorities (LEAs) individually decide what priority they give to the provision of adult literacy and basic skills. Adult Basic Education (ABE) in Scotland is overseen by the Scottish Community Education Council but provided regionally by the Community Education Service of LEAs.

45.   ALBSU, the BBC and the Training Agency are joint partners in a major literacy initiative for adults—the Basic Skills Accreditation Initiative. Launched in September 1989, this is a collaborative venture with new learning opportunities, encompassing BBC radio and television programmes, associated books and study materials, and new qualifications. Students will be able to work towards two certificates, awarded by City and Guilds, the first in communications skills and the second in numeracy.

46.   With funding from the Department of Education and Science of £1·1 million over three years, ALBSU has opened 10 Open Learning Centres in inner city areas. These provide adults with a variety of learning opportunities for improving inadequate literacy and numeracy skills, with particular emphasis on self-help through the use of new technology.

CHAPTER VII

Social Change and Children with Special Needs

Introduction

47.   The post-war years have seen dramatic improvements in the general health and welfare of children enabling the great majority of them to grow up to achieve their full physical, social and intellectual potential. However, these material improvements have also served to point up the special needs of children who, for reasons of health or circumstances, require support and protection to aid their growth and development. The Government has addressed these needs in the most comprehensive piece of legislation ever enacted about children in the United Kingdom—the Children Act 1989.

Child and Family Welfare

48.   The overriding purpose of the Children Act is to promote and safeguard the welfare of children within the context of the family. It includes:

*   new measures for protecting children from abuse—the Emergency Protection Order and the Child Assessment Order,

*   a range of " Section 8 " orders replacing custody and access orders to be available to the courts in family proceedings,

*   new emphasis on prevention and welfare services through partnership between parents and statutory and voluntary organisations aimed at enabling children and parents to influence decisions about themselves.

49.   A key provision is the duty the Act places upon local authorities to identify children in need and take appropriate measures to meet those needs. The Act defines a child in need as one who:

*   is unlikely to achieve or maintain a reasonable standard of health or development without the provision of services by a local authority; or

*   whose health or development is likely to be significantly impaired without the provision of such services; or

*   is disabled.

50.   The object is to exploit to the full the preventive potential of the surveillance and assessment activities undertaken by health, education and local authorities. Among those who will benefit from the provisions are children with disabilities, children at risk of abuse and children in families where matrimonial proceedings have implications for their care and custody. In Northern Ireland legislation similar to the Children Act 1989, designed to promote and safeguard the welfare of children, is being prepared. Scottish legislation, passed in a number of enactments, provides broadly equivalent measures to promote the welfare of children and their families, to protect children at risk and to care for children and families in need, and is currently under review.

51.   Policy on child protection issues has recently been revised to take account of the new legislative provisions contained in the Children Act. This built upon the Department of Health's multi-agency guide on the investigation of child abuse, "Working Together", which was first published in 1988. The main policy messages contained in *Working Together* are:

—the paramount importance of the welfare of the child;

—the importance of involving parents at every stage in child protection work;

—the importance of social workers developing effective interviewing skills;

—the need for specific agreed principles and policies for dealing with cases of organised abuse; and

—the need for advance planning to avoid inappropriate timing or unnecessary removal of children from their homes.

52.   Guidelines have been prepared on the investigation of child abuse which emphasise:

—the importance of selection and training of officers for this work, including the importance of effective joint training with professionals in relevant disciplines;

—the need for the police to participate with other professionals in a free exchange of information with a view to securing the child's best interests as early as possible in an investigation;

—the importance of multi-agency Area Child Protection Committees as a forum for developing, monitoring and reviewing child protection policies;

—the particular problems posed by allegations of organised abuse and the need for scrupulous observance of joint working procedures in such cases.

The Northern Ireland guidance on the management of child abuse "Co-operating to Protect Children", issued in 1989 and corresponding closely with "Working Together", will be revised to take account of the new legislative framework to be introduced by the forthcoming Children (Northern Ireland) Order.

Domestic Violence

53.   The problems associated with domestic violence span the interests and responsibilities of a number of Government Departments. Over recent years the Government has given a clear lead in initiatives to combat assaults against women. Work has been co-ordinated and taken forward through the auspices of the Ministerial Group on Women's Issues. Action to tackle the problem has included the publication in 1989 of research findings which provided a fresh insight into the problem and which formed the basis for a comprehensive plan of action; guidance in 1990 to the police and Crown Prosecution Service about improving the response to domestic violence; a review of the homelessness legislation and the long-term housing needs of victims of domestic assaults;

a review of the provisions of both the civil and criminal laws; the inclusion of relevant sex and family life education in health education programmes; moves to educate the public and raise awareness of the problems and needs of victims of domestic violence; and the encouragement of co-operation between local voluntary and statutory organisations to work together to provide help and support to women and children who are victims of domestic assaults. In Northern Ireland, a research project aimed at determining the most cost-effective methods of skilled intervention by Health and Personal Services staff in cases of domestic violence is being carried out during 1992.

Social Security for Families with Children

54.   For families with little or no other means of support, the Government provides cash help through income-related benefits: primarily Income Support, Housing Benefit and Community Charge Benefit. These benefits are built around a system of personal allowances and premium payments which make it possible to target resources on specific groups. There are personal allowances for children, according to age, and premiums for families and disabled children. The circumstances faced by lone parents, for example, are recognised through a lone parent premium and a more generous treatment of part-time earnings. The introduction of Family Credit enabled further significant progress to be made in directing resources to working families with children. In Great Britain, Family Credit now provides substantial tax-free weekly cash payments to boost the incomes of over 350,000 working families payable, in nearly every case, to the mother. The corresponding figure for Northern Ireland is 15,000.

55.   In recent years additional money has been put into the income-related benefits by increasing child allowances, and the family and lone parent premiums, over and above indexation in line with prices. In April 1990 extra help was announced for lone parents, low income families with disabled children and expectant mothers through social fund maternity payments.

56.   The Child Support Act 1991 will ensure that parents honour their legal and moral responsibility to maintain the children whenever they can afford to do so. The Act makes provision with regard to the assessment, collection and enforcement of payments of child maintenance. In large measure it removes from the courts the responsibility for assessing claims to child maintenance and varying existing orders. The Act also makes provision for maintenance awards to be calculated by formula. The formula will produce consistent and predictable results so that people in similar financial circumstances will pay similar amounts of maintenance. It will allow for maintenance payments to be reviewed regularly to keep up to date with the cost of living and so that changes in circumstances can be taken into account automatically. Changes will be made in the rules for social security benefits which are paid to people who are working, to make it easier for those who want to work to do so. The establishment of a Child Support Agency, to implement this Act, will help to provide many families with a more regular and reliable income.

Children with Special Educational Needs

57.   The Education Act 1981, and associated regulations, provides the statutory framework for special education in England and Wales. Similar legislation exists in Northern Ireland. It abolished the previous statutory categories of handicap as the basis for special education and placed the emphasis instead upon identifying the individual child's special educational needs. The appropriate special educational provision to meet those needs is then decided. The Act established a sound national framework for progress within which Local Education Authorities (LEAs) have been able to develop their own local policies for meeting local needs and circumstances. The statutory system of assessment which it has put into place gives parents clear rights of involvement at all stages and offers them significant rights of appeal against the decisions of their LEAs, including to Ministers.

58.   LEAs are required by the Act to educate children with special educational needs in ordinary schools subject to the views of the child's parents, and provided that this is compatible with their receiving the special educational provisions they require. The provision of efficient education for the other children with whom they are to be educated and the efficient use of resources are also taken into account. Because of these changes,

more children are being educated in ordinary schools who would in former times have been placed in special schools. The position is much the same in Scotland, though education authorities are encouraged, rather than obliged, to educate children with special educational needs in mainstream schools.

59.   The Government's policies under the Education Reform Act 1988 are designed to build upon and enhance the progress achieved by the 1981 Act. The National Curriculum offers all children, including those with special educational needs, a common entitlement to a broad and balanced curriculum. Teachers in special and ordinary schools will now share a common curriculum base and a common set of benchmarks, and this will enhance greatly the possibilities of the transfer of pupils from special schools to ordinary schools and help integration. The greater freedom given to schools, including special schools, to control their own budgets under schemes of Local Management will improve the quality of education for children with special educational needs. Similar policies apply in Northern Ireland as a result of the Educational Reform (NI) Order 1989. In Scotland, the 5–14 Development Programme provides guidelines covering the main areas of the curriculum and, as in England and Wales, children with special educational needs must be given full access to it.

Juvenile Delinquency

60.   The Government recognises the importance of protecting children from the harmful consequences of delinquency, and the Children Act 1989 puts a general duty on local authorities to prevent children becoming involved in offending. Parents have the main responsibility and opportunity to ensure that their children do not turn to crime. Some need support, and the 1989 Act also puts a duty on local authorities to ensure that families have access to advice, guidance, counselling and other relevant services. The Government encourages, fosters, and in some cases provides, funds for local crime prevention initiatives, many of which are targeted on young people. Most young people who offend grow out of crime. To encourage this process of development the Government's policy is that juvenile offenders should be dealt with in the community wherever possible. In recent years there has been a significant increase in the population of juvenile offenders who are cautioned (ie given a formal police warning) rather than prosecuted. The number of juveniles given custodial sentences has fallen from about 3,000 in 1982 to less than 2,000 in 1990.

61.   In Scotland there is a different system for dealing with young offenders—the children's hearings system. The central feature of this system is that it places an even greater emphasis on dealing with children in the community while protecting the rights of child and family by allowing them recourse to the courts on appeal. A unique feature of the system is that it deals not only with young offenders under the age of 16 but also with children who have been offended against and who are perhaps victims of neglect or abuse. Since 1980 there has been a slow but steady drop in the number of referrals on offence grounds with a concomitant increase in referrals for other reasons.

62.   The Children Act does not apply to Northern Ireland. There the relevant legislation, currently under review, is the Children and Young Persons Act (NI) 1968. However, the Government and its appointed agencies operate on the basis of the same philosophy as regards juvenile crime prevention and dealing with offenders in the community, and Health and Social Services Boards are required to provide services aimed at reducing the need to bring children and young people before the courts.

AIDS and Drug Misuse

63.   The United Kingdom Government attaches the highest priority to confining the spread of AIDS/HIV infection which has the most serious implications for the health and welfare of both children and adults. Government action includes a health education programme aimed at increasing awareness of high risk activity, and health care and social welfare support both to people suffering from the condition and their families. The Government is also co-operating in international initiatives concerned with the treatment and prevention of AIDS/HIV. It is absolutely central to Government policy that, across all aspects of their education, care and treatment, children with AIDS/HIV are seen as children first and are not unnecessarily deprived of the opportunities for growth and development available to children generally.

64.   The use of illicit drugs by children under 14 years is thought to be rare in the United Kingdom. But the Government is committed to ensuring that young people are made aware of the harmful effects of drugs and are equipped with the knowledge, skills and attitudes they need to resist pressure to misuse them within the context of an overall programme of preventive health education which emphasises the positive benefits of a healthy lifestyle. *All* maintained schools are now required to provide education about drugs as part of the National Curriculum.

65.   The Government is setting up local drug prevention teams to strengthen community resistance to drug misuse in selected areas considered to be most at risk from drugs. Their activities will be largely directed to protection of young people from drug misuse, by developing preventative strategies with youth workers, schools and, not least, with parents.

66.   Children can, of course, be adversely affected by parental drug misuse. An increasing number of drug misusers are women, and the Government has issued guidance to health authorities to ensure that the planning of drug services takes into account the special needs of pregnant women and mothers with young children. Increased funding is being provided by the Government for the development of residential services for drug misusing mothers with their children.

CONCLUSION TO PART I

67.   The British Government welcomes the World Summit for Children's role in focusing attention on the welfare of children. The completion of a follow-up report to the Summit has been useful in this respect, and the United Kingdom hopes that other countries will also have found it a useful exercise. The United Kingdom Government will continue to give the highest priority to providing good quality schooling, health care and family support for our nation's children.

PART II: UNITED KINGDOM OVERSEAS ACTION

Through the United Kingdom Aid Programme

Introduction

1.   The Declaration on the Survival, Protection and Development of Children agreed at the 1990 Summit committed all those present to work to improve child health and security, to enhance the role of the family, to develop appropriate education, to mount an attack on poverty, and to protect the environment. All of these issues are basic concerns of the British aid programme administered by the Overseas Development Administration (ODA).

2.   The fundamental aims of the British aid programme are to promote sustainable economic and social development, to reduce poverty and to encourage good government—ie to help poor countries help themselves in achieving self-sustaining growth and developing their societies in their own way. The promotion of human development, including better education and health, and supporting programmes that allow women to have children by choice, is an essential element of the programme. The targets of ODA's poverty-focused aid are poor households, with particular reference to women. Aid directed towards these targets benefits children in ways that are sustainable over the longer term.

The Policy Environment

3.   The Plan of Action for the implementation of the World Summit's Declaration highlights the need for alleviation of poverty and revitalisation of economic growth to meet and sustain the goals for long-term child survival, protection and development. It also stresses the need to address abject poverty and hunger which attack children as the most vulnerable segment of Society (paragraph 24).

4.   Although decisions on aid priorities must of course take account of the fact that Britain is dealing with sovereign governments and must therefore take account of their priorities and development plans, certain overall priorities exist. ODA concentrates aid on the poorest countries and uses it in ways which are the most likely to achieve a reduction in poverty that can be sustained. About 80 per cent of British bilateral aid goes to countries with average incomes of less than $700 per head, and 70 per cent to the poorest 50 countries. It alleviates poverty by:

—planning poverty reduction projects in all major aid recipient countries;

—supporting multilateral initiatives to improve the poverty reduction policies and programmes of aid recipient countries;

—developing the competence of ODA staff in this area, by seminars and improved guidelines;

—debt reduction packages, eg, initiatives proposed at the Commonwealth Finance Ministers' meeting in Trinidad in September 1990.

5.   These initiatives have to be set in a policy context conducive to their success. British aid promotes economic reforms in developing countries in order to:

—promote trade liberalisation and foreign exchange reform, helping governments reduce distortions to prices and inefficient practices;

—encourage better public expenditure programmes, especially those concerned with the provision of basic social and economic services. These include education, health and water.

6.   The ODA seeks to protect vulnerable groups from hardship during economic reform. It has encouraged the World Bank to incorporate social and gender considerations into its structural and sectoral adjustment credits. As part of this initiative, a social development adviser has been seconded to the Social Dimensions of Adjustment programme in the Bank. The structural adjustment process must be undertaken with an eye to the need for longer-term development to improve the quality of human life. Short–term programmes to investigate the transitional costs of adjustment, however necessary, are no substitute for reviving those long-term social programmes which contribute most to the desirable reduction of poverty.

7. Economic success depends not only on freer, more open economies, but also on good government:

—the implementation of sound economic policies, providing open, accountable and competent administration, absence of corruption and avoidance of excessive military spending;

—observance of human rights and the rule of law;

—legitimacy and accountability, freedom of expression, political pluralism, broad participation in the development process.

Improving the quality of government thus affects poor people both directly and indirectly. Those hitherto excluded from the development process as politically and economically marginal ultimately stand to benefit the most.

8. Paragraphs 26 and 27 of the Plan of Action stress that children have the greatest stake in the preservation of the environment. At the beginning of 1991 over 2,000 forestry projects were in progress or in preparation at a cost of £170 million. The British Government is helping developing countries limit their contributions to global warming through our energy efficiency initiative. It has committed around £40 million as part of a new programme to improve the Global Environment to help developing countries tackle problems such as climatic change and the loss of the biological diversity of our plant and animal species. It has also integrated environmental concerns into all aspects of our developmental planning.

British Aid Expenditure in Sectors likely to Affect Child Survival, Protection and Development Directly or Indirectly

9. *The Bilateral Programme*

This section shows expenditure in those sectors of the aid programme most likely to affect children, breaks this down into activities of especial relevance to the World Summit for Children's goals and illustrates, through examples, the kind of activities undertaken and sets this within the context of United Kingdom policies and strategies.

10. *Project Aid and Technical Co-operation*

Social and Community Services Sector. Most identifiable bilateral aid expenditure of direct relevance for children consists of project aid and technical co-operation. Total expenditure, in recent years has been as follows:—

TABLE 1

Bilateral Social and Community Services Expenditure 1988–1990 (£000s)

Sector	1988	1989	1990
Health and Welfare	27,584	31,316	38,224
Water and Sanitation	21,462	25,903	24,779
Education	88,727	92,743	103,860
Public Administration	21,201	25,612	32,693
Urban and Industrial Development	6,866	8,649	4,342
Housing	1,010	1,325	1,195
Other Community Services	120	233	633
Total	**166,970**	**185,781**	**205,726**

The following sections review ODA actively in Health, Water and Sanitation and Education, showing how these expenditures are benefiting children.

19

Health

11.   The ODA is actively engaged in supporting the development of health care services in over 20 countries, taking account of people's actual needs when the projects are being designed. Objectives include:

—strengthening primary health care services;

—improving control of communicable diseases;

—helping to establish systems for managing health services, so that they provide good quality care at an affordable cost; and

—improving access to reproductive health services.

Expenditure over the last three years is at Table 2.

12.   The Summit's Plan of Action refers to the increasingly serious effect that the AIDS pandemic is having on children's prospects in developing countries. The United Kingdom has been a major contributor to the WHO's Global Programme on AIDS and to national AIDS control programmes. It is presently reviewing ways in which it can further strengthen the impact of its assistance in this area.

13.   Rapid population growth is one of the key development problems of the 1990s: it acts as a brake on developing countries' economic progress, and prevents alleviation of poverty; it puts the health of women and children at risk; and it increases pressure on natural resources and the environment. The ODA is committed to trying to ensure that reproductive health services in developing countries meet the demands of couples who want to choose when to have children. Direct assistance to population programmes amounted to some £24 million in 1990, a 28 per cent increase in real terms over 1989. In August 1991 the ODA launched an initiative which will further strengthen support to population programmes over the next two years. Eight Asian and African countries will receive significant additional assistance to their national population programmes over this period. The aim is to help improve the coverage and quality of reproductive health services in these countries, improve the reliability of contraceptive supplies, and enable women to take greater control over their lives and exercise reproductive choice.

TABLE 2

Health Expenditure 1988–1990 (£)

	1988	*1989*	*1990*
Total	27,289,339	30,845,670	38,024,295

14.   A considerable part of health project expenditure relates to the strengthening of primary health care, including local clinics and dispensaries as well as hospital services. Over 30 per cent of technical co-operation expenditure on health was devoted to family planning and population activities, reflecting the priority which ODA attaches to these areas. Support to mother and child health, primary health care, social welfare community services and nutrition also feature among activities having a direct impact upon children.

Examples of Health Sector Projects

15.   While ODA does not normally specifically target children under aid projects, the well-being of children has always been central to the British aid programme. The reduction of infant and child mortality and morbidity levels is a particular priority of ODA health sector assistance, whether under its bilateral or multilateral programmes or through its support to NGOs under the Joint Funding Scheme. Women's health is a further priority, and this directly benefits their children too.

16.   The ODA's largest mother and child health (MCH) project is in the Indian state of Orissa, where £25 million is being spent on the second phase of a project to strengthen MCH services in 19 districts covering 25 million people. Once the project is completed in 1993 it will have constructed 2,000 health centres, trained 3,000 auxiliary nurses and midwives, and upgraded management of the state's health services generally.

17.   Children, and through them their parents, are the target of a schools health project in Andhra Pradesh. The ODA is collaborating with the Indian Ministries of Education and Health to introduce the concepts of preventive health and health education into the curriculum for eight million five to 11 year olds throughout the state. Health workers and teachers will be trained to work together to treat common problems such as anaemia, diarrhoea, and worms, and to identify hearing and sight disabilities which may impede a child's progress. Health messages will be carried out of the classroom in interactions with the community.

18.   The Integrated Family Welfare and Rural Development Project, Gujarat, is jointly funded and run by an Indian NGO. The infant mortality rate in villages covered by the project has dropped from 130 per 1,000 in 1981 to 85 per 1,000 in 1988. The project also seeks to reduce maternal mortality rates through improvements in pre-natal and post-natal care for mothers.

19.   One of the aims of the Indore Slum Improvement Project, India, is to improve levels of maternal and child health in parallel with physical improvements to the slum areas of Indore. One specific target, for example, is to achieve an 80 per cent immunisation rate among pregnant women and an 80 per cent delivery of births by trained attendants in the areas covered. The project also aims to eliminate malnutrition among children in the slum population through an integrated approach to urban development which structures health inputs into wider social and economic development.

20.   The ODA is providing substantial support to programmes for the control of malaria, which kills at least one million victims each year, most of them children. In Kenya, the ODA has been advising the government on a National Strategy for Malaria Control. Ways in which services can be improved, with donor assistance, are being investigated. In Gambia, the ODA funds the United Kingdom Medical Research Council's laboratory which is testing new treatments for malaria and other diseases. It is also helping national malaria control programmes in India, Bangladesh, Sri Lanka, Cambodia, Zimbabwe and Namibia.

21.   ODA is also involved in working to reduce diarrhoea, a major cause of child mortality in developing countries. As well as bilateral projects, ODA supports the International Centre for Diarrhoeal Disease Research in Bangladesh and also the WHO's special programme on Diarrhoeal Diseases Control.

22.   Health and educational needs of women are particularly addressed in the ODA's Women in Development Strategy which aims to integrate attention to women's needs into all aid activity. An example of how this approach operates and meets targets for improving matrilineal skills is:—

—the Hindustan Fertiliser Corporation Rainfed Farming Project (£3·25 million over six years commencing in 1988–89) which seeks to develop a low cost participatory approach for agricultural development in rainfed areas of eastern India. The project is designed to encourage and support the full participation of women farmers. The improved nutritional skills of women and children is identified as one of the key indicators of achieving the project's immediate objectives—the adoption of appropriate technologies for different agro-ecological zones.

Water and Sanitation

23.   In the last three years ODA project and technical co-operation assistance for water and sanitation has been as follows:

TABLE 3

Water and Sanitation—Expenditure 1988–1990 (£'000s)

1988	1989	1990	Total
21,462	25,903	24,779	72,114

Water Supply

24. Activities in this sector must cover a range of needs. The ODA's schemes run from large and conventional projects such as that in Lahore, Pakistan, to the Senegal Rural Water Supply Project or the Five Towns Project in Ghana. Projects have also helped to provide rural borehole supplies in Uganda, and operational and maintenance support to large-scale supplies in Madras, India. In Nepal, ODA has helped with the construction of small town supplies in Eastern Nepal, and in Mauritius and St Lucia it has helped in leak detection and the management and operation of the water utilities.

Sanitation

25. Of equal importance is the removal of foul water and solid waste. Help has been given to the improvement of conventional water-borne sewerage systems in Cairo, Egypt, and Lahore, Pakistan. Many parts of the developing world cannot yet afford such systems, however, and alternative safe systems such as improved pit latrines are provided in many areas of Southern Africa and Asia. Surface water drainage systems also need improvement and this is especially important in the poorer, often lower-lying and less well-drained sections of many developing country cities. Lack of solid waste disposal and garbage collection can provide breeding-grounds for insects and vermin. In crowded and low-standard housing these are significant carriers of disease. Once again it is the poor and the young who are especially at risk, and increasing attention is now being focused on appropriate collection and disposal systems.

Education

26. Recent expenditure on projects and technical co-operation is shown on Table 4.

TABLE 4

Education Expenditure 1988–1990 (£)

	1988	1989	1990
Education*	57,627,154	57,139,921	61,593,086
Materials and Curriculum Devt	245,951	430,433	1,124,093
Inspection and Management	302,931	450,522	598,273
Educational Buildings	2,178,346	1,586,457	1,367,268
Education Equipment/Materials	4,238,420	5,074,313	4,601,809
Primary Education	1,425,373	1,071,432	1,677,851
Secondary Education	7,817,248	10,111,674	8,219,475
Universities	4,123,966	4,479,497	4,851,820
Tertiary Technical Institutions	4,126,569	4,566,212	5,595,720
Teacher/Adviser Training	1,953,746	2,797,988	4,387,516
Primary Teacher Training	26,459	4,664	103,657
Secondary Teacher Training	914,125	1,368,271	2,218,280
Distance Learning	910,812	1,109,671	1,790,307
Technical Education	989,688	972,786	1,466,078
Nursery Schools	215,438	228,752	341,471
Adult Education and Literacy	397,087	277,332	946,693
Research/Scientific	872,520	461,138	2,235,097
Total	**88,365,833**	**92,131,063**	**103,098,489**

* Almost entirely, British Government Training and Scholarships Schemes.

27. ODA's approach to education in developing countries seeks to complement national efforts to improve education. There is a continual assessment of how investment in education in recipient countries should be divided between the various levels: primary, secondary and tertiary. There are also demands for investment in continuing education, particularly adult literacy and skills upgrading for those not completing formal education.

28. The weight of recent evidence demonstrates that investment in young children at primary level yields the best economic returns, although investment in children at secondary level may be almost as effective. There has been a significant shift in ODA assistance towards support for primary education projects and support to the provision of learning materials and books.

29. By the end of the 1980s approximately 70 per cent of education project aid expenditure was directed towards primary and secondary education. This represents a marked shift away from investment in tertiary education which characterised earlier years. Spending on technical co-operation in education accounts for about a third of all technical co-operation expenditure. Concern is not only with the numbers of children involved but also with the quality, efficiency and effectiveness of their education. ODA has therefore been closely involved with teacher training and the production of programmes and teaching materials. Educational projects are supported by the ODA only where they can deliver demonstrable improvements in raising the skills necessary to achieve sustainable human resources development.

Examples of Education Projects

30. ODA is increasingly involved in primary and pre-school education. For example:—

The Indore Slums Project seeks to ensure that 60 per cent of three to five year olds receive pre-primary education, and that 75 per cent of those in pre-primary education enrol in primary school. The project also focuses on school drop-outs and on adult education.

By far the most ambitious project is in Andhra Pradesh, India, where a seven year project aims to train 150,000 teachers from 50,000 primary schools in child-centred active learning techniques and build primary schools at a cost of £35 million to provide an attractive learning environment for children.

A five year project in Kenya is designed to raise the quality of primary education through emphasis on human resources including teachers, teacher trainees and inspectors.

31. Education is not an end in itself and must link with other aspects of development such as Nutrition. ODA is supporting pre-school education where young children are not only provided with educational experiences but are fed and cared for while their mothers receive training in nutrition and health care. Such day care or pre-school centres have an important spin-off for older sisters who are often kept away from school in order to look after younger brothers and sisters.

32. ODA has a particular focus on improving female literacy and it is sensitive to the fact that the organisation of classes, the techniques used and the materials provided may have to be amended in particular circumstances to ensure that women benefit from literacy training. In all projects where it is appropriate, consideration is given to the inclusion of a female literacy component. Examples of current project activity aimed at reducing adult illiteracy which incorporate special needs of women are:—

—through the Indo-British Fertiliser Education Project (ODA allocated £34·92 million) materials are being produced to meet the needs of illiterate women farmers;

—the ODA support for the non-formal education project, part of the Government of Ghana's Programme of Action to Mitigate the Social Costs of Adjustment, is aimed at providing literacy for women, especially schoolgirls.

Literacy is linked to other projects such as clean water, primary health care and the provision of skills for income-generation.

Non-Governmental Organisations (NGOs)

33. ODA support for the NGO sector currently totals about £88 million, around half of which goes towards emergency relief, and half towards longer-term development projects. The ODA funds NGOs' work overseas in three main ways: through the Joint Funding Scheme, through the British Volunteers Programme and through Emergency Relief Aid, including disaster, refugee and food aid.

Joint Funding Scheme

34.   As part of its bilateral technical co-operation expenditure, the ODA provides grants to voluntary organisations through the Joint Funding Scheme (JFS). Under the JFS the ODA provides 50 per cent of the cost of agreed specific projects and the NGO provides the corresponding 50 per cent. Any British NGO involved in development work overseas is eligible for funding. The British government provides block grants to five of the larger NGOs, four of whom have the welfare of children high on their priority list. These four NGOs are Christian Aid, Oxfam, Save the Children Fund (SCF) and the Catholic Fund for Overseas Development (CAFOD).

TABLE 5

**ODA Expenditure on Children-related Projects Under the JFS
1988–89—1990–91**

Year	No. of Projects	No. of Agencies	Total Spent
			£000s
1988–89	61	12	2,135
1989–90	79	12	2,654
1990–91	72	13	2,060
Total	**212**		**6,849**

The projects funded can be broken down into the following types:—

—Education: schools, special education, creches and pre-school education

—Health: immunisation, nutrition/feeding, Primary Health Care (PHC) and Mother and Child Health (MCH) programmes

—Children in Especially Difficult Circumstances: street children, drug addicts, orphans, young offenders, child protection centres, physical disability, mental handicap, lepers.

The bulk of the JFS expenditure goes to projects in the health/immunisation/feeding area, directly supporting a number of the goals contained in the Summit's Plan of Action.

35.   Britain also works closely with NGOs in the field of project implementation, particularly in tackling poverty within local communities leading to obvious benefits for women and children.

36.   Two projects of particular interest approved in 1990 were based on working with NGOs that are precisely aiming for sustainable models of rural development. One, in Pakistan, was a grant of £4·8 million through the Aga Khan Foundation for a second phase of its rural support project in the remote Chitral District of northern Pakistan. Following a successful initial phase supported by a £3·7 million ODA grant made in 1987, it will seek among other things to develop an apex organisation which will be able to deliver services to the local communities in future without the need for continued injections of aid. Similarly, a £7·8 million grant to the Bangladesh Rural Advancement Committee will support the latter's development programmes, including the establishment of a special bank to provide credit on a self-sustaining basis. Both projects are also supported by other donors.

Britain's Volunteer Programme

37.   The ODA provides up to 90 per cent of the income of four British agencies responsible for the recruitment of volunteers to work in developing countries. The main recipients of assistance under this scheme are Voluntary Service Overseas (VSO), the Catholic Institute for International Relations (CIIR), Skillshare Africa and the United Nations Association International Service (UNAIS). The ODA provided £14·295 million in 1990–91 and £15·890 million in 1991–92 for this purpose. There are nearly 1,500 volunteers working in over 50 countries, many of them in sectors such as Health, Education and Community Services.

Multilateral Aid

38.   About 40 per cent of United Kingdom aid is channelled through multilateral institutions such as the World Bank, the EC and the United Nations agencies. Many major development strategies can be pursued more effectively by multilateral institutions than by individual donor countries operating on their own. Multilateral institutions are often valuable centres of expertise. These include the World Bank for economic reform and the UNFPA for population expertise.

39.   The British contribution to the four United Nations agencies whose work is most closely associated with the goals set out in the Summit's Plan of Action—UNICEF, WHO, UNFPA and UNHCR/UNWRA—was £56·175 million in 1990. In addition to core funding contributions to UNICEF, contributions are also made to their work in emergency situations; these sums are not included in the above figure.

Emergency Relief Aid

40.   There are very few emergency relief efforts which do not substantially touch the lives of women and children. ODA responds to a large number of natural and man-made disasters and to the plight of the world's 15 million refugees, with food, money and material help. In 1990 it provided over £70 million in humanitarian assistance world wide.

41.   In April and May 1991 the Minister for Overseas Development announced two new allocations of humanitarian aid for Africa, together worth £50 million. This brings the total of such aid to £110 million in response to the present crisis and to £230 million since the beginning of 1989, including our share of EC aid. Of this, over £204 million has gone to the six worst hit countries and almost £130 million to Ethiopia and Sudan combined.

Research

42.   In 1989–90 £48 million was spent on research which amounts to some 3 per cent of the overall costs of the aid programme. Priority in research is given to work with direct relevance to the poorer sectors of poor countries, with particular reference to the rural sector.

43.   ODA is giving increased attention to research on a number of health issues of particular relevance to children including reproductive health, malaria, AIDS, disease control, nutrition, diarrhoeal diseases, and child mortality. Other subjects include longitudinal study of young children, urban youth, substitute care policies, female participation in education, low cost housing and sanitation.

Other Programmes

44.   The programmes described above are those where there is tangible direct benefit for children in developing countries. They cover only part of aid expenditure. The rest of British aid also benefits children, but indirectly, through benefits to improve living standards and quality of life.

ANNEX A

Crown Dependencies

Jersey, Guernsey and the Isle of Man are not part of the United Kingdom, but are dependencies of the Crown, each with its own legislature and executive, including its own child care administration. The Crown Dependencies are all considering their position in relation to the World Summit for Children document and to the United Nations Convention on the Rights of the Child. They are also considering whether they wish any of the provisions of the Children Act 1989 to form part of their own legislation.

ANNEX B

Dependent Territories

Each Dependent Territory pursues its own policies to look after its child population which vary considerably in size from Territory to Territory. All inhabited Dependent Territories have been sent copies of the World Summit Declaration and Plan of Action in order that they might take this into account when setting objectives and allocating resources.

To complement the United Kingdom's domestic follow-up to the Summit, the Dependent Territories were asked to provide information about the kinds of programmes and policies they pursued in each of the main areas targeted by the Summit. The following is a summary of contributions received:

(a) *Child Health*

Infant and under-five mortality rates are monitored in each Dependent Territory and nowhere exceed 50 and 70 per 1,000 respectively and are typically very much lower. There is a wide provision of basic health services with immunisation high on the list of priorities; in Hong Kong for example immunisation coverage for babies born in 1990 was 99·8 per cent against tuberculosis, 90·9 per cent against diphtheria, pertussis and tetanus, 92 per cent against poliomyelitis and 88·4 per cent against measles, mumps and rubella. In Anguilla and the Falkland Islands, immunisation rates are as high as 95 per cent.

Dependent Territories are encouraged to develop their own plans for tackling health problems etc; Montserrat has recently proposed a " Maternal and Child Health Plan " for the period 1992–96. St Helena is developing a system for the regular collection of health data to monitor levels of health and health care provision. Its health plans already target diseases with a high incidence rate, such as asthma, allergic rhinitis and congenital defects. Anguilla is about to implement a school health programme aimed at the early identification of child health problems.

(b) *Maternal Health*

Pre- and post-natal services are widely available for women and have resulted in generally low maternal mortality rates—recently zero in the Falkland Islands and Turks and Caicos Islands. Most births take place in clinics or hospitals. Access to health education and family planning services is also good. Birth control devices are available free to all from the Medical Department in the Falkland Islands. Throughout, education and counselling about family planning, as well as availability, are regarded as important to make these services effective.

(c) *Nutrition*

Malnutrition is not a serious problem in any of the Dependent Territories. More commonly, territories have focused on problems such as *excessive* sugar consumption leading to tooth decay. Montserrat and St Helena are among those who have made recent efforts to tackle dental disease. Nutrition continues to be monitored for potential problems; in the Turks and Caicos Islands, for example, a public health nurse was allocated in 1988 to be solely responsible for the nutritional status of school children.

(d) *Basic Education*

Free universal primary education is available in each Dependent Territory, with equal access for girls and boys. Many provide secondary education as well. A particular problem for several of them is the provision of education for those living in sparsely populated areas. The Falkland Islands and Anguilla have both developed the provision of " distance learning " education to cope with this.

In some of the territories with the most sophisticated education systems, there is also provision for children identified as having special educational needs. In Hong Kong such children are integrated as far as possible, though placed in special schools when their handicaps are such that they cannot benefit from the ordinary school programme. In St Helena there is also a special educational needs programme.

Where adult illiteracy occurs, it is generally among the older sections of the population who did not benefit from the introduction of universal education. Most Territories provide some adult education, for example, Hong Kong provides formal and non-formal education for adults, and Turks and Caicos Islands provides extension classes in English and literacy classes for adults. Anguilla has appointed a teacher to look into adult education including a possible literacy programme for adults.

(e) *Water and Sanitation*

Provision of safe drinking water and sanitation facilities varies between the Dependent Territories. Hong Kong has achieved 99·8 per cent of the population with access to safe drinking water and 95 per cent connected to a public sewer (remainder with septic tanks). The Turks and Caicos Islands have identified the improvement of the quality and availability of bulk water supply as a priority, and aid monies from the British Government are being used for this purpose. The Pan-American Health Organisation is proposing a project to construct a limited number of pit latrines in the poorest areas of the Islands to improve sanitation.

(f) *Special Circumstances: Vietnamese Migrants*

Hong Kong, in addition to looking after its own children, has for some time been looking after the Vietnamese migrant children on the Islands in the best way possible. All the detention centres in Hong Kong have well-equipped clinics which provide the Vietnamese population with free medical care. Any Vietnamese migrants in need of hospital services are admitted to hospitals outside the camps.

It is ensured that all Vietnamese migrants are well nourished; the dietary scales in use have been carefully drawn up by Government dieticians in consultation with UNHCR technical advisers. Despite the limited space available in the detention centres, camp managements have made major efforts to provide Vietnamese children with open space for recreation as far as possible.

Unaccompanied minors are placed under the guardianship of the Superintendent of the centre in which they are detained. In order to make their lives in the centres as normal as possible, suitable foster parents are sometimes found by voluntary agencies for these children. A Special Committee has been set up by the UNHCR to advise the Hong Kong Government on the status and durable solutions appropriate to each of these children.

ISBN 0-10-119842-6

9 780101 198424

Printed in the UK by HMSO
2176 Dd 0301984 C7 6/92 3218490 19542